Year **2**

Adult • Quarter 3

God's Justice and Mercy

STUDENT GUIDE

> Forever, O LORD, Your word is settled in heaven. Your faithfulness endures to all generations; You established the earth, and it abides.—Psalm 119:89–90

GOD'S WORD FOR ALL GENERATIONS

Answers
BIBLE CURRICULUM

Contents

Introduction 5

1   Kings of Israel and Judah 7
    Prepare to Learn 8
    Studying God's Word 11
    A Worthy King 12
    God's Word in the Real World 14
    Prayer Requests 14

2   God Warns Israel 15
    Prepare to Learn 16
    Studying God's Word 19
    God Is 19
    God's Word in the Real World 20
    Prayer Requests 20

3   God Loves Israel 21
    Prepare to Learn 22
    Studying God's Word 25
    Children of God 25
    God's Word in the Real World 27
    Prayer Requests 28

4   God Judges Israel 29
    Prepare to Learn 30
    Studying God's Word 32
    Sorting Out Syncretism 32
    God's Word in the Real World 36
    Prayer Requests 36

5   God Judges Nations 37
    Prepare to Learn 38
    Studying God's Word 41
    Jonah Meets Nahum 41
    God's Word in the Real World 42
    Prayer Requests 42

6   God Speaks Clearly 43
    Prepare to Learn 44
    Studying God's Word 47
    God vs. Nostradamus 48
    God's Word in the Real World 49
    Prayer Requests 50

7   God Answers Prayer **51**

Prepare to Learn 52

Studying God's Word 55

In God We Trust 55

God's Word in the Real World 56

Prayer Requests 58

8   The Coming Ruler **59**

Prepare to Learn 60

Studying God's Word 63

Mining for Truth 63

God's Word in the Real World 65

Prayer Requests 66

9   Messianic Prophecies **67**

Prepare to Learn 68

Studying God's Word 71

The Old Testament Cross 71

God's Word in the Real World 73

Prayer Requests 74

10   God Warns Judah **75**

Prepare to Learn 76

Studying God's Word 79

Idols of the Heart 79

God's Word in the Real World 80

Prayer Requests 80

11   God Judges Judah **81**

Prepare to Learn 82

Three Steps to Destruction 85

Studying God's Word 86

God's Word in the Real World 87

Prayer Requests 88

12   Seventy Years **89**

Prepare to Learn 90

Studying God's Word 93

Is Context King? 93

God's Word in the Real World 95

Prayer Requests 96

Introduction

As we continue our study of Old Testament history, we will continue to see the nation of Israel rebel against the Lord. Time and time again God sent them prophets to call them to repentance and to warn them of coming judgment. But over and over, the kings and the people ignored God's words and continued in their disobedience and idolatry. So finally, God's judgment came. But even in the midst of God's judgment we see His mercy.

In addition to warning God's people and proclaiming His coming judgment, many of the prophets also gave hope and comfort to God's people. One way they did this was by telling them of the coming Messiah—the one who would ultimately give His life as an offering for sin.

When you think about it, we are really not that different from the Israelites. We don't worship statues and carved images today, but we are prone to worship many other things than God—to put things and people ahead of Him in our lives.

If we are belieers, we should be overflowing with gratitude that God's judgment has been taken away by Christ—that the punishment due to us for our sin and rebellion has been paid on our behalf. What a wonderful message that we have to share with those around us!

We encourage you to read the Prepare to Learn section before class each week. This will provide important background information so that you will get more from each lesson.

For more information and links to online articles, be sure to visit the Online Resource Page at www.AnswersBibleCurriculum.com.

Kings of Israel and Judah

1

Key Passages

2 Chronicles 10:13–19

- **Israel:** 1 Kings 14:7–18, 16:25–28, 16:29–33; 2 Kings 10:30–31, 17:1–2

- **Judah:** 2 Chronicles 12:1, 12:12–14; 1 Kings 15:8–15, 22:41–44; 2 Kings 18:1–10, 24:17–20

What You Will Learn

- The pattern of the kings of Israel and Judah.

Lesson Overview

The nation of Israel was judged by God because of Solomon's sin of idolatry. After his death, God used Solomon's son Rehoboam and his foolish actions to judge Israel. Israel was split in two. The wicked line of kings led the people in Israel and Judah away from the Lord. God judged them again using the Assyrians and the Babylonians who overthrew the nations and scattered the people.

Memory Verse

Isaiah 42:8

I am the Lord, that is My name; and My glory I will not give to another, nor my praise to carved images.

 **Prepare to Learn**

SCRIPTURAL BACKGROUND

What a mess! As we look at the history of the kings of Israel and Judah after the death of Solomon, we can't describe it any other way. Israel had existed as a united kingdom for about 120 years during the reigns of Saul, David, and Solomon, but the kingdom was torn in two and never restored. To truly study all of the details of the two kingdoms would take a very long time, so the goal of this lesson is to give a quick overview of the two kingdoms. We will take a specific look at the kings and prophets in the North and how that kingdom finally was taken captive to Assyria (2 Kings 17:5–6) in 721 BC. Then we will look to the Southern Kingdom—briefly reviewing the history that ended with its final destruction by the Babylonians (2 Kings 25:1) in 588 BC. As you read and study the Scripture passages, you will notice the kings of Judah and Israel are described as either doing good or evil in the sight of the Lord.

In Scripture, the Northern Kingdom is referred to as Israel or Ephraim. The Southern Kingdom is called Judah most of the time, with a few exceptions. The capital of the Northern Kingdom was originally in Shechem and later moved to Tirzah and then finally to Samaria. Throughout the books of First and Second Kings and Second Chronicles, we find accounts of the persistent wickedness of the 19 different kings who ruled in Israel—the worst being King Ahab and his queen Jezebel (1 Kings 16:33). The wickedness started with King Jeroboam I in 975 BC, and God revealed that these kings of the North (Israel) failed to worship Him and led the people astray with the worship of false gods (1 Kings 14:7–10). Altars and high places were constructed to worship false gods along with idolatrous Ashtoreth poles and temples for Baal worship. It was a dark time for Israel as there were no kings that sought to honor the God who had given them the Promised Land as an inheritance.

Throughout over 200 years of these evil kings reigning in Israel, God sent His prophets—like Amos, Hosea, and Elijah—to call the people and the rulers to repentance. However, the kings and their people refused to return to God, seeking their own power and pleasure rather than God's glory. And so, finally, God acted in judgment by bringing the Assyrian army against them. In 721 BC, the capital of Israel, Samaria, fell and the people were taken captive (2 Kings 17:5–6). The Northern Kingdom was no more.

The kings of the Southern Kingdom, Judah, followed a different pattern. Rehoboam followed his father, Solomon, on the throne, and the line of David continued to rule in Jerusalem in fulfillment of God's promise to David (2 Samuel 7:13–16). Rehoboam angered the people and was cruel to them as he sought to establish his name rather than God's (1 Kings 12:10–11). His son Abijam (also called Abijah) continued in this tradition of cruelty and idolatry (1 Kings 15:3). Then came Asa, Abijam's son. He cleansed Judah of the idols and the perverted persons (1 Kings 15:11–14). Next was Jehoshaphat, who walked in the ways of his father, Asa (1 Kings 22:43). Jehoram, the son of Jehoshaphat, then began to reign in Judah. He did not walk in the way of his father Jehoshaphat, but followed the ways of the wicked kings of Israel and did what was evil in the sight of the Lord. This began a cycle of good kings/bad kings in Judah, continuing through all 20 kings of the Southern Kingdom.

As with Israel, God sent various prophets to Judah to proclaim His judgments and call the people to repentance. Judah was much more responsive to God's call, but most of God's warnings and calls to repentance were not heeded. Through all of the messages of coming judgment and calls for repentance, God knew that He would ultimately have to execute judgment against His children. Just as the Northern Kingdom, Israel, had fallen to the Assyrians in 721 BC, Jerusalem was to fall at the hands of the Babylonian King Nebuchadnezzar (2 Kings 25:1). This would be the end of Judah as an established nation and the beginning of a period of control by the empires that would rule the Middle East over the next centuries.

As we look back over this history, we should be gripped by the patience of God to continuously send His messengers to call for repentance—over hundreds of years. We should also look soberly at the judgment that God sent against Israel and Judah and know that we face God's chastening if we sin and rebel against Him. As Christians, we need to be listening to the message God has given to us through His completed Word.

HISTORICAL/APOLOGETICS BACKGROUND

Sadly, looking at the Northern and Southern Kingdoms of the children of Israel, you won't find them to be much different than the kingdoms that were around them. The two kingdoms warred against one another throughout their history. Not unlike the professing church in America today, there was much corruption and hypocrisy in Israel and Judah. You might think humanity would learn from these lessons of history, but it seems that we keep repeating the same mistakes over and over.

Outside of Israel and Judah, the Greek culture was developing, and the first Olympiad was held in 776 BC. Homer and Aesop were writing the classics of Greek literature, and, on the other side of the globe, the Mayan culture was blooming in Central America. In general, this period of history could be described as one of constant upheaval, accompanied by the rise and fall of major empires.

Despite all of the uncertainty and turmoil in the world, God was still reigning over everything, just as He is today. This is an important fact that we must keep in the forefront of our minds. God is still just as much in control of the world today as He was then. This is a truth that can help us understand how to live in the world today. It doesn't matter who is president or what country is invading which—we must fix our hope on God and what He has done for us on the Cross. Just as Paul exhorted the Christians in Colossae, we must set our minds on the things above, where Christ is seated at the right hand of God, and not on the things on the earth (Colossians 3:1–4).

Confidence that God is sitting on His throne with Jesus at His right hand offers us great comfort and hope. We can rejoice in His goodness, knowing that He is patient to call sinners to repentance as they look to Christ for forgiveness.

For more information on this topic, see the Online Resource Page.

 **Studying God's Word**

Will there ever be a worthy king?

Take notes as you study the following passages about the kings of Israel.

1 Kings 14:7–18, 16:25–28, 16:29–33; 2 Kings 10:30–31, 17:1–2

Take notes as you study the following passages about the kings of Judah.

2 Chronicles 12:1, 12:12–14; 1 Kings 15:8–15, 22:41–44; 2 Kings 18:1–10, 24:17–20

 # A Worthy King

Just as the Israelites followed the lead of the kings of Israel and Judah, we often follow the lead of those who are placed in authority over us. We also actively follow those we choose to allow to influence us as we listen to teaching, watch movies, read books and blogs, and listen to music. Knowing that we live in a fallen world and that each of these authorities in our lives is fallen and sinful (to various degrees), we need to carefully consider how we act in light of those influences. Consider the following questions about the authorities in your life and examine your heart to identify any sin or idolatry you need to deal with, keeping in mind that influence can be positive or negative.

1. If someone influential started to worship idols, would it be right for you to worship those idols?

2. Think about the areas of faith, finances, friendship, lifestyle, music, entertainment, etc. Who are the people (whether you know them personally or not) that you consider to be influential in your life in these different areas? Whom do you choose to associate with, allowing them to influence you?

3. Which of the influences above are godly? Which have an ungodly influence?

4. Read 1 Corinthians 11:1. Why was Paul worthy of influence in the life of the Corinthians?

5. Read 1 Corinthians 15:33–34. Which of the influences you listed above (also consider books, movies, internet, and other sources that you allow to bring ideas into your mind) are corrupting you and leading you away from holiness?

6. The Israelites typically rejected the message of the prophets God sent them—calling them to repent and turn back to worshipping God rather than the idols. How do you typically respond when people come to you with rebukes pointing out sin in your life and calling you to repent?

7. The Israelites, including the kings, had some access to the written commands of God and to the hearing of God's truth through the prophets. How do you respond when you read God's Word and recognize your sin?

Take time during this week to prayerfully read and meditate on Ephesians 5, asking the Holy Spirit to show you where there are corrupting influences and godly influences in your life. Confess any sin to God, knowing that you are forgiven in Christ, and then seek to put off the ungodly influences and put on the godly influences by the power of the Holy Spirit.

God's Word in the Real World

1. When you read these passages about kings who worshipped false gods and idols, do you tend to think of yourself as capable of committing that type of sin or as being better than those silly idolaters?

2. In the passages we read, there were many legacies described as one person was said to have walked in the ways of someone before him, whether good or bad. What are the major ways that you are seeking to leave a godly legacy to those who will follow you as you follow Christ (1 Corinthians 11:1)?

3. If you have identified some sinful tendencies after our activity, what things can the people in this room do to come alongside you to bear that burden and bring restoration through forgiveness in Christ (Galatians 6:1–5)?

4. In light of what we have studied today, why is it so important to keep our eyes fixed on Christ as our true King?

Prayer Requests

2

God Warns Israel

Key Passages

- Amos 2:6–12, 3:1–2, 3:9–11, 4:10–12, 5:4–7

What You Will Learn

- The content of God's message to Israel through Amos.

- The attribute of God that demands judgment.

Lesson Overview

The Lord sent the prophet Amos to the northern kingdom of Israel to deliver a message of judgment. Through Amos, the Lord warned Israel to turn to Him or He would send an adversary to destroy them. God showed His patience with Israel, but He must judge sin.

Memory Verse

Isaiah 42:8

I am the Lord, that is My name; and My glory I will not give to another, nor my praise to carved images.

Prepare to Learn

SCRIPTURAL BACKGROUND

In the opening verse of the book that bears his name, Amos is identified as a shepherd from Tekoa, a small town about nine miles south of Jerusalem. Amos was a simple man, caring for sheep and growing sycamore figs (7:14), and God used this humble man to communicate a message of pending judgment to the Northern Kingdom of Israel. Amos was one of many prophets sent by God who were rejected by the people of Israel.

As a prophet, Amos delivered his message as straight from God. Throughout the book, Amos recorded exactly as God directed. The phrase "says the Lord" appears in this small book over 40 times! There is no doubt here that God was the source of the message—as He was the source, through the Holy Spirit, of the writing of all Scripture.

Amos was faithful to deliver the message from God, which not only warned of coming judgment because of Israel's sin and disobedience (Amos 2:13–16), but also offered forgiveness and grace to the people if they would repent (Amos 5:4, 5:6, 5:14–15). God would finally punish their sinfulness, but He gave Israel decades to repent—revealing His patience.

Ultimately, Amos's message was rejected—even by Amaziah, the priest who accused Amos of conspiring against the king. The priest reported Amos to the king and told the prophet to flee to the land of Judah and never again prophesy in Israel (Amos 7:10–13). God warned that an army would come against Israel. An adversary would be all around the land, sap their strength, and plunder the palaces (Amos 3:11). Israel did not listen, and this judgment came upon them when the Assyrians captured and deported the people of Israel in 721 BC (2 Kings 17:5–6).

The Old Testament prophets are divided into two groups—major prophets and minor prophets. Amos is considered one of the minor prophets, but that certainly doesn't mean that he was less important or that his message was less significant than any of the other prophets. The classification of "minor" primarily refers to the length of the book in our Bibles.

The books of the minor prophets do NOT appear in chronological order in the Bible. For example, Amos was prophesying long before Ezra and Nehemiah, whose lives are recorded in the Bible before the book of Amos. Likewise, Isaiah prophesied after Amos, yet his writings appear in the canon before the book of Amos. This is something to be aware of as you pursue Bible study. The books of the Bible are not arranged chronologically, but are arranged by sections. Knowing this will help you to discern, through careful observation of all of Scripture, what the historical context is—not only of the major and minor prophets but of all biblical history as well.

The prophets of the Old Testament had many roles. Amos fulfilled two of those roles by delivering messages of judgment to God's people and to foreign nations—both Israel and the Gentiles. Chapter 1 confirms this when we read that Amos delivered the message of God's wrath against the Gentile nations of Syria, Philistia, Tyre, Edom, Ammon, and Moab. Then, using the same language, he focused on Judah and then at length on Israel. God spoke with the same certainty against the Gentile nations as He did against His own chosen people. The Bible tells us that "God is angry with the wicked every day" (Psalm 7:11). But though God's justice knows no partiality, He had mercy on those who turned to Him in repentance and faith. And He is still willing to freely pardon all those who repent and place their trust in the Messiah—Jesus Christ (Acts 10:34–38).

HISTORICAL/APOLOGETICS BACKGROUND

The introduction to the book sets Amos during the reigns of Uzziah, king of Judah, and Jeroboam II in Israel. Interestingly, Amos mentioned that his message was delivered two years before the earthquake. Throughout Scripture we find that earthquakes often accompanied God's judgment. So what earthquake was Amos referring to? Apparently, he assumed the readers would know which earthquake he was talking about. As we compare Scripture with Scripture, rightly dividing the Word of truth, we find a similar reference in Zechariah 14:5. And, though not specifically recorded in Scripture, the Jewish historian Josephus reported an earthquake accompanying God's judgment on Uzziah when he offered incense to God in the Temple. We read in 2 Chronicles 26:16–22 how Uzziah had sinned against God by entering the Temple to perform a duty assigned to the priests.

As we read and study Scripture, we need to keep in mind that, although historical information is great confirmation of what the Scriptures tell us, the records of men like Josephus are not inspired by God. Josephus was a reputable historian, and it is a reasonable possibility that the earthquake occurred when God struck Uzziah with leprosy and was the same earthquake mentioned by Amos.

As God surely promised in Amos 3:11, Israel did eventually fall to an adversary. That adversary was the nation of Assyria, who under the leadership of Shalmaneser V besieged Israel's capital city of Samaria (2 Kings 17:1–8). God's patience with the 10 tribes of the

Northern Kingdom had ended, and His justice was enacted through the destruction of their capital and the deportation of the people. Ten tribes of the 12 were now scattered among the nations. Now only two tribes (Judah and Benjamin) remained to the south in the nation of Judah. But it would not be long until Jerusalem and Judah would suffer the same fate as the nation to her north.

For more information on this topic, see the Online Resource Page.

 ## Studying God's Word

Complete this sentence: "God is . . ."

Take notes as you study the following passages.

Amos 2:6–12, 3:1–2, 3:9–11

Amos 4:10–12, 5:4–7

 ## God Is . . .

Discuss the questions posed by your teacher after listening to the script.

God's Word in the Real World

1. What parallels do you see in the book of Amos and our culture today?

2. In what ways are we called to act like Amos in our culture?

3. Are there any areas in which you think you have been influenced by the "God is love" movement?

4. What hope do you have in overcoming false ideas about God that you may believe or have believed?

5. Knowing that judgment is certain for every sinner, why is understanding the gospel and who Jesus is so important?

6. God was patient with the Israelites and gave them, as a nation, hundreds of years to repent and turn back to Him before He destroyed them. How have you seen God's patience in judgment in your life or others who are close to you?

Prayer Requests

3
God Loves Israel

Key Passages

- Hosea 1:1–2:1, 3:1–4:3, 11:1–11; Romans 5:6–8

What You Will Learn

- How God loves Israel despite their rebellion.

Lesson Overview

The book of Hosea is a unique account of the prophet Hosea, his wife Gomer, and her unfaithfulness. This love story of Gomer and Hosea is compared to God's faithful love for Israel. In spite of their rebellion and turning to false gods, God loved them and was willing to forgive them. God's love for His people will not end but He will not share His glory with another.

Memory Verse

Isaiah 42:8

I am the Lord, that is My name; and My glory I will not give to another, nor my praise to carved images.

Prepare to Learn

SCRIPTURAL BACKGROUND

Hosea described one of the most shocking portrayals of God's relationship with His children. God compared His relationship with His children to a marriage with a prostitute who would not remain faithful. These are strong and bitter words through the mouth and actions of a prophet. They must have rung sharply in the ears of the people of Israel. And as the people witnessed Hosea take Gomer as his wife, observed Gomer leave Hosea for other men, and then watched as Hosea tenderly took Gomer back in love and forgiveness, the message that God meant to convey to His people became even clearer. Just as Gomer had abandoned her husband for other lovers, so had Israel turned from the one true God to false gods and idols (Hosea 2:2–13). And just as Gomer's husband bought her back from slavery, so God brings His children back in mercy and love.

The mercy and love of God is put on display in the book of Hosea in a way that is glorious. It is easy to love the lovable or to offer gifts to those who will return the favor, but it can be oh so difficult to offer forgiveness to those who have stolen from you or violated your trust in the most intimate of ways. That is the very thing God called Hosea to do when he was told to buy Gomer back from the slave market where she had landed and to love her (Hosea 3:1–3). In this act, God portrayed His relationship with the adulterous Israelites. God was willing to show mercy; God was willing to take them back again.

Israel surely deserved God's wrath for their constant violations of His commands. God would have been just in wiping out the nation for their sins, but He had made promises to Abraham and David to bring the Messiah from the nation of Israel. His mercy was shown in withholding punishment—He didn't give them what they deserved (though later He would). In fact, His love was demonstrated as He restored them in spite of their sin and their rejection of His authority.

God spoke of Israel as a child He had raised (Hosea 11:1), lovingly guiding Israel from their bondage in Egypt into the Promised Land where He lavished His child with blessings and care. As a loving father, God would administer discipline to His child as Assyria brought destruction and captivity, but it grieved God to have to do it (Hosea 11:5–8). However, God would not utterly destroy Israel forever, and He promised His people the hope of restoration in the future. If they would again walk after the Lord, the Lord would take them back and let them dwell again in their houses (Hosea 11:9–11).

God offered a call of repentance from seeking after idols and trusting in the gods and kings of other nations. However, Israel did not respond to His call. He promised to heal their backsliding and love them freely. He wanted them to turn from their gods and trust in His mercy (Hosea 14:1–4). In the end, if His children would return, they would be revived and grow in the Lord (Hosea 14:8). The wise would recognize that He is a merciful God and the only God worthy of their worship. The future restoration of Israel (see section below) would demonstrate God's love for those who are truly His children.

The parallels between the book of Hosea and the lives of Christians today are not difficult to see. We are born in sin, and God is dishonored by our disobedience, rebellion, and idolatry. Yet God has purchased us with the price of His Son from the slave market of sin (Ephesians 2:1–10). We have been brought from pursuing our own selfish interests to pursuing the righteousness of Christ. And when we backslide, God uses discipline to bring us back to Himself (Hebrews 12:5–14). This book demonstrates God's unconditional mercy and love to His children as Hosea reunites with his wife and reconciliation occurs.

And the account reminds us of the unconditional love of God offered to us through Jesus Christ. We have rebelled and deserve only His wrath and justice because of that rebellion. But God is faithful and merciful to forgive, through Jesus Christ, those who humbly repent and turn from their sins. What a glorious God we serve, what an amazing message we have to share, and what a responsibility and privilege God has given us to convey this message to the next generation.

HISTORICAL/APOLOGETICS BACKGROUND

Hosea was a contemporary of Isaiah, Amos, Nahum, and Micah. He prophesied in the Northern Kingdom of Israel through the reigns of four kings of Judah (Hosea 1:1). Though he prophesied for more than 60 years, Hosea is still considered one of the minor prophets for his relatively short book. In his writing, Hosea refers to Israel as Ephraim and Jacob interchangeably. Ephraim was one of the tribes that had settled in the north after the conquest. When the Northern tribes had wholly abandoned the worship of the true God, they fell under the control of the Assyrians. This was what God warned His people of through Hosea (Hosea 11:5). And it was only about 75 years after Hosea began prophesying that Samaria (the capital of Israel) fell to the Assyrian king and God's chastening began for the Northern Kingdom.

Within Hosea's prophecies are clear references to the future restoration of Israel. Exactly when that restoration will occur is a point of debate among sincere believers. Some see the promises made to Israel as unfulfilled and pointing to a period when the nation will be restored to the Promised Land. Particularly, this is often connected to the millennial reign depicted in Revelation as a period of peace (Hosea 2:16–20). In general, those who hold a premillennial view of Christ's Second Coming would understand these passages as looking to the future restoration of Israel as a nation. Those who take an amillennial view typically see these passages as prophetic imagery and not as actual events that will take place. Amillennialists believe the events will be fulfilled as Christ returns to initiate the eternal state, but not in a distinct 1000-year period. While these are important ideas to seek answers to, we must be charitable to those who come to different conclusions than ours, providing those conclusions are based on Scripture alone. Regardless of our view on this particular subject, we know that God is faithful to His promises, and we can trust that the warnings present in Hosea's writings are still relevant today. We are to worship God alone, trust in Him alone, and put our faith in Christ alone.

For more information on this topic, see the Online Resource Page.

Studying God's Word

How does God show His love?

_____

_____

Take notes as you study the following passages.

Hosea 1:1–2:1, 3:1–4:3

_____

_____

_____

_____

Romans 5:6–8

_____

_____

_____

Children of God

Read the following scriptures and answer the questions.

1. John 1:10–13—What makes someone a child of God?

2. Romans 8:16–17—Who is the "we" pointing to as being children of God?

3. Hebrews 12:5–8—What marks a legitimate child (son) of God?

4. Who is contrasted with the children of God in the following three passages?

   • Philippians 2:14–15

   • 1 John 3:1–3

   • 1 John 3:8–10

   Additional Notes:

   • Colossians 1:13–14

   • Ephesians 1:3–6

5. So, who is a child of God?

Take notes as you study the following passages.

Hosea 11:1–11

Matthew 2:15

 God's Word in the Real World

1. What imagery in this passage of Scripture has helped you to understand God's love in a fuller way or corrected a misconception you had?

2. How could you use this concept of being a child of God to encourage a fellow believer who is suffering as a result of clear sin in their lives?

3. While there is a sense in which all people are "children" of God—He has created everyone—how has this idea become distorted in our culture, and how can we help to correct the misunderstanding?

4. How can you use the truths you have heard today from Scripture to share the hope of Christ with someone?

Prayer Requests

God Judges Israel

4

Key Passages

- 2 Kings 17:1–18, 17:24–41; Amos 3:11

What You Will Learn

- How God brought judgment to Israel.

- The source of tension between the Jews and Samaritans.

Lesson Overview

For 250 years the people of Israel did what was right in their own eyes—turning their backs on the Lord. So the Lord used the Assyrians to judge Israel. Assyria besieged the walled city of Samaria and conquered Israel. They then scattered the people and moved foreigners in to occupy the land.

Memory Verse

Isaiah 42:8
I am the Lord, that is My name; and My glory I will not give to another, nor my praise to carved images.

📖 Prepare to Learn

SCRIPTURAL BACKGROUND

God warned the people that judgment would come (2 Kings 17:13–18). He spoke through His prophets Hosea, Amos, and others. The time had come. Israel was about to be wiped out as a nation and carried away into captivity for their unwillingness to turn from their sin and trust in God.

The 10 tribes of Israel suffered as a result of the wicked kings who led the people to idol worship away from the true God. The suffering was a result of spiritual famine. They had gotten to the place where only a small remnant remained committed to honoring God. The others feasted on their selfish lusts and made their offerings and sacrifices to false gods.

Over time, the leaders did not cling to the truth of the Creator God who alone was to be worshipped. Politics and power became the driving force, and alliances were made with the surrounding nations. In disobedience and rebellion, they turned from the One who had brought them out of Egypt. Worship had been corrupted, and even the priests of God were participating in idol worship. Rather than a sweet-smelling aroma (Philippians 4:18), the worship of the people was a stench in the nostrils of God. In fact, Israel looked a lot like many Western countries today.

God was patient for 250 years, sending many prophets to warn Israel and Judah. But after years of consistent rebellion, idolatry, sin, and hostility toward God, His anger was finally provoked to action, and He judged Israel by removing them from His sight (2 Kings 17:18). The Lord finally rejected Israel, afflicted them, and delivered them into the hand of plunderers (2 Kings 17:20). God sent the powerful nation of Assyria to bring judgment upon the nation that had forsaken Him. The Northern territory would never be fully under the control of Israel again. The Promised Land had been torn from them because of their unfaithfulness.

God proves Himself patient and gracious to all of His followers. We all were once alienated and enemies of God by wicked works. Yet He offered us reconciliation through the death of Jesus Christ. This miracle of salvation presents those who trust in Christ as holy, blameless, and above reproach before our holy God (Colossians 1:21–22).

Just as many perished in Samaria, many more will perish eternally one day because of their sin. The judgment on Israel will pale in comparison with that final judgment. We are called to be ambassadors on behalf of Christ, imploring people to turn from their sin and trust in Christ (2 Corinthians 5:20–21). The gospel is the only truth that can save. It is the only truth that can bring the hope and peace we all seek.

HISTORICAL/APOLOGETICS BACKGROUND

As the capital of Israel, Samaria was the site of the final showdown between Assyria and the Israelites in the North. Shalmaneser V had taken tribute from Hoshea, but Hoshea turned against him to the king of Egypt (2 Kings 17:3–4). Shalmaneser wouldn't stand for that, so he conquered the land of Israel. However, the takeover of Israel's capital, Samaria, took three years. Why so long? As a fortified city, Samaria had its own supply of food and water within the walls. The Assyrians unglamorous yet effective plan of attack was to set up camp outside the city and wait until the people inside starved or opened the gates.

The siege lasted through the reign of Shalmaneser V, and some believe that he died at the end of the campaign. After the land was fully taken, the Assyrians conducted a campaign of relocation. The Israelites were delivered to the regions of Halah, Habor, Gozan, and the cities of the Medes (2 Kings 17:6). These were regions far to the east in modern-day Iraq, Syria, and Iran. However, many of the poor and non-threatening Jews were left in Israel to work the land.

As the Assyrians conquered more lands, they settled Samaria with the foreigners from those lands (2 Kings 17:24). The new citizens moved in, and with them came their worship of false gods. They did not fear the Lord or know how He demanded to be worshipped (2 Kings 17:25–26). And, as always, this angered God.

In response to God's judgment of sending marauding lions, the foreigners sent for a priest in the hopes they could learn the rituals of the true God and so appease His anger (2 Kings 17:26–27). But God demands nothing short of perfect obedience and worship of Him alone. And although the priest did show them how to worship God, they continued to make gods of their own and put them in the shrines. The worship continued to be blended in perverse ways, and God was not honored (2 Kings 17:28–33). In addition, the Jews intermarried with these foreigners and they became the Samaritans, whom the Jews despised but Jesus reached out to (John 4:1–42).

Here we can see a clear present-day principle to apply from this Old Testament passage: Beware of churches that integrate worship practices from religions around the world. This type of syncretism promotes a false worship of God. This is unacceptable. We are to have no false gods before us. We are to love the Lord our God with all our hearts, our minds, and our souls.

For more information on this topic, see the Online Resource Page.

 **Studying God's Word**

Can we worship God however we want to?

Take notes as you study the following passages.

2 Kings 17:1–23

Amos 3:11

2 Kings 17:24–41

 Sorting Out Syncretism

Throughout the history of Israel, the Jews had repeatedly blended the religious practices of the false gods of the surrounding nations with the worship of Yahweh—the true God. Read the following information about yoga and certain meditation practices with the goal of deciding whether these practices should be used by Christians to worship God.

Yoga

How would you describe yoga?

In an article published in *The New York Times*, a Hindu organization lamented the loss of the Hindu identity of yoga in the West:

> Organizers of the Take Back Yoga effort point out that the philosophy of yoga was first described in Hinduism's seminal texts and remains at the core of Hindu teaching. Yet, because the religion has been stereotyped in the West as a polytheistic faith of "castes, cows and curry," they say, most Americans prefer to see yoga as the legacy of a more timeless, spiritual "Indian wisdom."
>
> "In a way," said Dr. Aseem Shukla, the foundation's co-founder, "our issue is that yoga has thrived, but Hinduism has lost control of the brand."

Some of the earliest written records of yoga practices are contained in the Bhagavad Gita. These Hindu scriptures were delivered in part by the god Krishna. In chapter 2, Krishna tells another god, "Be steadfast in yoga, O Arjuna. Perform your duty and abandon all attachment to success or failure. Such evenness of mind is called yoga." The various forms of yoga are intimately tied to the practices of "salvation" in Hinduism, Buddhism, Jainism, and other Eastern religions.

The various positions (asanas) taken in physical yoga are intended to connect the individual with the divine nature of the universe, to channel energy centers in the body, and to offer worship to various gods. An explanation of some of the yoga postures follows:

> Yoga may be approached as a way to keep your body fit and healthy, but the true meaning of yoga is deeply

rooted in spiritual enlightenment. As you stretch, contract and contort your body, you're engaging in an ancient ritual, which is meant to cleanse your body and soul. By understanding the spiritual meaning for the various poses that you use in yoga, you'll have a better understanding of why each individual pose works together to give you that post-workout high.

Sun Salutation—The 12 distinct poses of the Sun Salutation each has their own mantra and the series is meant to celebrate the sun and the sun god.

Animal Poses—The spiritual purpose of each animal pose is to allow you some of the attributes that each animal possesses. For instance, the eagle pose is said to bring you a clear mind's eye and a lion's pose can help you feel brave and in control. (Jae Ireland, "Spiritual Meanings of Yoga Postures," Livestrong, http://www.livestrong.com/article/395082-spiritual-meanings-of-yoga-postures.)

1. Should Christians seek to merge themselves with the divine nature of the universe?

2. Does the Bible ever direct us to use certain physical postures to help us find peace or to gain the character traits of part of the creation?

3. Should Christians seek to practice a part of the Hindu religion, knowing that we are to do all things to the glory of God (1 Corinthians 10:31)?

Meditation

How would you describe meditation?

_____

_____

Certain forms of meditation are part of the practice of yoga and other Eastern religions like Buddhism, Jainism, and Sikhism. The goal in some of these meditation practices is to empty the mind so that a connection with the divine nature of the universe can be made. Other practices are intended to connect to spiritual guides or to channel energies from various gods or regions of the body.

4. What is the focus of meditation in Joshua 1:8 and Psalm 119:15?

5. Does God ever call us to empty our minds to connect to Him?

6. Should Christians be seeking to empty their minds in order to understand Christ more fully?

God's Word in the Real World

1. How can we relate God's patience in bringing judgment to Israel to sharing the gospel with unrepentant people today?

2. Why is syncretism, blending worship practices into Christianity, so dangerous?

3. Where have you seen God's patience in bringing judgment in your life or others?

Prayer Requests

5

God Judges Nations

Key Passages

- Nahum 1:1–15, 2:1–3:19

What You Will Learn

- The source of the message of Nahum.

- How the books of Jonah and Nahum are connected.

Lesson Overview

The Lord's wrath burned against the wicked Assyrians. But before He destroyed them, He sent His prophet Nahum to the capital, Nineveh, to warn them of God's judgment. The people would not repent like they had when Jonah came 100 years earlier. So God used another nation to destroy Nineveh and the Assyrians.

Memory Verse

Isaiah 42:8
I am the Lord, that is My name; and My glory I will not give to another, nor my praise to carved images.

 **Prepare to Learn**

SCRIPTURAL BACKGROUND

God works throughout history to accomplish His plans. Nineveh arose as the capital of the powerful nation Assyria. Assyria was a growing power in the region and had taken control of a major portion of the Middle East. God was aware that Nineveh was a wicked city and that evil was pervasive throughout the empire. In His kindness to the heathen nation, God sent Jonah to proclaim a message of judgment against Nineveh and the Assyrians (Jonah 1:2). Jonah's message was received by the people of Nineveh. Even the king responded in repentance (Jonah 3:6–9). God saw that they had turned from their evil ways, and in His mercy, He spared the city (Jonah 3:10).

Their affection for God and His laws did not last long, however. Within 100 years, Nineveh had returned to idolatry. The king at that time was seeking to magnify his own name over God's.

Enter Nahum—at a time in history when Assyria, at the height of its power, was hated and feared by all nations. God used Nahum to deliver a prophecy of doom concerning Assyria: "The Lord has given a command concerning you: 'Your name shall be perpetuated no longer. Out of the house of your gods I will cut off the carved image and the molded image. I will dig your grave, for you are vile'" (Nahum 1:14). God hated the cruelty, sin, and idolatry of the Assyrian nation and was about to smash it.

So now God's judgment was coming on Assyria because of their wickedness and sinfulness. But wait a minute! God was going to judge Assyria for her cruelty and sin, and yet they carried out His will, His judgment on the Israelite nation when they conquered the Northern Kingdom. It had been God's plan that Assyria overthrow Israel and deport them. It doesn't appear just that God would then turn around and judge the Assyrian nation who carried out His will against Israel.

But God can do no wrong. His plans are perfect, and whatever He does is fair and just and righteous. Although we often don't understand what He does in the Bible and throughout history, we must never accuse God of doing wrong. As Abraham said to God before He judged Sodom, "Shall not the Judge of all the earth do right?" (Genesis 18:25).

The Israelites willingly rejected God and turned to worshipping false gods—their judgment was just. The Assyrians willingly attacked another nation and took it captive, fulfilling their own evil desires for power. Each side sinned, and God used this sin to accomplish His plans without sinning Himself. We could say that God uses sin sinlessly. Just as God warned Israel to return to Him but judged them by sending Assyria to conquer them when they refused to repent, He then used Nahum to warn Nineveh of coming judgment. They chose not to repent, so God judged them by sending another nation, the Babylonians, to satisfy His judgment on them.

Under the leadership of Nabopolassar, the Babylonians rose and conquered the Assyrians about 100 years after they had overthrown Israel. This occurred only about 25 years after Nahum's writing and prophecy of this very judgment.

In most cases throughout the Bible, the judgment delivered by God came at the hand of other people. He delivered the message through people and brought the judgment through people. We are aware, of course, of notable exceptions where God sent fire from heaven (Genesis 19:24) or flooded the entire earth (Genesis 7:17), but God typically acted through people.

Again, let's remember that God can do no wrong. Although we may not always understand how and why God does certain things, He is always faithful to His own character. He cannot sin, and He always conducts His plans on the earth in a just way— in a manner that brings glory to Himself (Romans 11:36). God is in control, and we can absolutely rest in knowing that the God of all the earth does what is right—His own righteous, unchanging character demands that.

HISTORICAL/APOLOGETICS BACKGROUND

Placing Nahum in the history of Israel is a bit more difficult than most of the other prophets. For example, Amos opened his book with a detailed list of the kings in Israel and Judah reigning at the time of his prophecy. But Nahum didn't give us that historical context. We can, however, be certain of some things. Because Nahum spoke of Assyria and Nineveh in their glory, his prophecy must have been written at a time when Assyria was prospering. Up until the end of the reign of Ashurbanipal, who ruled Assyria from 668–648 BC, Assyria prospered. We also know that Nineveh was overthrown by Nabopolassar in 626 BC, which was the judgment Nahum prophesied about.

The other interesting tidbit in the text is that Nahum calls himself an Elkoshite, indicating where he might be from (Nahum 1:1). There are several different possibilities for this location. One is Al Qosh in Iraq, so it is possible that Nahum or his parents were among those exiled from Israel in 721 and resettled in the north of the Assyrian territories. With all of this in mind, Nahum likely delivered his prophecy against Nineveh around 650 BC at the height of Assyria's power. God used a nation that He prospered to bring judgment upon

Israel. And eventually, that nation would be overthrown by the Babylonians who would capture Jerusalem, taking the remainder of God's people captive.

Remember, only about 150 years passed from the time of Jonah—when the entire city of Nineveh repented—to Nahum and his prophecy. And the fall of Nineveh came only about 25 years after the prophetic proclamation from God through Nahum.

What a reminder of how quickly an entire nation can rebel against God. Or a family! Or a person! Because God is jealous for His own name, He will not leave unbelief and rebellion unpunished. Only in Christ does anyone have hope of being forgiven of rebellion against God. God shows His kindness in sending a call to repentance in the face of judgment (Romans 2:4). Also, Jesus has shown us the kindness of God by placing Himself in our place—trading our sins for His perfection. What a glorious truth to proclaim to others and to cherish in our own hearts.

For more information on this topic, see the Online Resource Page.

 ## Studying God's Word

How does God bring judgment?

_____

_____

Take notes as you study the following passages.

Nahum 1:1–15

_____

_____

Nahum 2–3

_____

_____

_____

 ## Jonah Meets Nahum

Although the two men never met (Jonah was around over 100 years before Nahum), they were used by God in very similar ways. For each of the categories below, identify the similarities in the two accounts of these prophets as they were used by God.

1. Compare the actions of Jonah and Nahum.

2. Compare the messages of Jonah and Nahum.

3. Compare Nineveh's response to Jonah's and Nahum's messages.

4. Compare God's response to Nineveh in each account.

 ## God's Word in the Real World

1. As we think of the message of judgment, why is it important to identify the source of the message?

2. How does making connections between Jonah and Nahum help you understand God's plan of redemptive history?

3. In what ways do you struggle with the "fairness" of events in history in light of the attributes and character of God?

4. How could you use the connection between Jonah and Nahum as a way to disciple a new believer or someone who is having difficulty trusting God's Word?

 ## Prayer Requests

6
God Speaks Clearly

Key Passages

- 1 Kings 13:1–7; 2 Kings 23:15–20; Isaiah 44:28–45:7; Ezra 1:1–4

What You Will Learn

- The timing and details of the prophecy of Josiah.

- The timing and details of the prophecy of Cyrus.

Lesson Overview

God knows all things—past, present, and future. He revealed specific future events in the Bible through His prophets and each of those events came to pass exactly as He intended. Unlike people who make vague prognostications or use a "might" phrase to trick people, God speaks clearly and there is no doubt of His omniscience.

Memory Verse

Isaiah 42:8
I am the Lord, that is My name; and My glory I will not give to another, nor my praise to carved images.

 **Prepare to Learn**

SCRIPTURAL BACKGROUND

Old Testament prophets had many different functions. They delivered messages of coming judgment to the Jews, told of pending destruction of foreign nations, called people to worship God rather than idols, received and communicated truth about God and His character, and delivered messages to individuals about specific situations. And sometimes, they told of future events, such as giving glimpses of the life and ministry of the Messiah. When you mention that someone was a prophet, most people think that he told of the future. While this is one part of a prophet's role, we need to be careful not to put too much emphasis on the future-telling role of a prophet—that was only part of his job.

With that preface, one of the most dramatic confirmations of the Bible's truthfulness is the specificity of the future-telling prophecies of the Old Testament. While some prophecies are somewhat vague, others give such clear detail that there is no doubt that they could ever be the result of "coincidence." Some details of future events are increasingly revealed as time goes on. We see the first hints of a Savior in Genesis 3:15, and later prophets proclaimed more details about His coming. Jacob told us He would come from the tribe of Judah (Genesis 49:10); Micah told us where He would be born (Micah 5:2); and Isaiah told us how He would suffer and die (Isaiah 53).

God was displaying His omniscience for our benefit. God knows everything that ever has happened or ever will happen. He was not making some guesses about what might happen some day or hoping that someone would read what was written and do it. God was demonstrating His absolute power and knowledge about the future. What an amazing gift God has given to us in His Word. He has graciously allowed us to see His character to know that He is in control. When we place our trust in God, we trust the God who is in control—knowing the future and directing it to His ends.

Jeroboam was the first king of the 10 Northern tribes. Shortly after taking power, he made two calves for Israel to worship, along with altars, so the people didn't have to worship in Jerusalem (1 Kings 12:28–33). Jeroboam had no interest in serving God in a faithful way, but he sought to blend the worship of God with false gods. He appointed priests who were not from Aaron's line, and he led the people into idolatrous adultery. Jeroboam set a feast day to initiate his new system of worship, offering sacrifices to the calf gods at Bethel. The sacrifices and incense burned on the altars were about to rise up before the Lord—but He was not pleased. He was no more pleased with this than when His chosen people worshipped the calf Aaron had made for them (Exodus 32).

God sent a prophet to pronounce judgment on Jeroboam and Israel. An unnamed prophet ("a man of God") went from Judah to Bethel, and he cried out with God's judgment against the king. Twice in the opening verses of 1 Kings 13 we read the phrase "by the word of the Lord." The message communicated by the prophet came from God through the lips of a man. The words delivered were words that had both immediate and future fulfillment.

As Jeroboam cried out against the prophet, God made his hand wither and the altar was split, spilling the ashes of the detestable sacrifices, just as the prophet had proclaimed (1 Kings 13:3). God used an immediate miracle to authenticate the message of the prophet and assure the future prophecy. In verse 2, God revealed that a king named Josiah would be born to the house of David and he would confront the spiritual adultery in Israel—killing the adulterous priests and burning the bones of dead men on the altars.

In order for this prophecy to be fulfilled, there would have to be a king by the name of Josiah born from the house of David. He would have to kill the high priests who were offering at the high places and then burn the bones of dead men on the altars. Well, that is exactly what happened 300 years after Jeroboam had his adulterous feast day. As we look at 2 Kings 23:15–20, we see this prophecy about the future fulfilled to the letter by a king named Josiah—a true testament to the omniscience of God.

Another amazing foretelling comes through the mouth of Isaiah. About 150 years before the Jews were to return from their exile in Babylon, Isaiah spoke of a king named Cyrus, whom God would prosper and then use to send the people back to Jerusalem to begin its rebuilding (Isaiah 44:28–45:7). Providentially, a king named Cyrus rose to power in Persia, overthrowing Babylon and allowing the Jews to return. As Ezra records, the Lord stirred up Cyrus to make a proclamation that the Jews should return to Jerusalem and rebuild the Temple (Ezra 1:1–4). Not only did he allow them to return, but also he gave them riches and commanded others to support them!

From the creation of the universe, God has been in absolute control of all that He created. Not only does God know who He will place in power in the future, but also He guides the hearts of those kings like channels of water. Stop for a moment and thank God for revealing His omniscience and sovereignty to us.

HISTORICAL/APOLOGETICS BACKGROUND

Since they reject supernatural events, liberal theologians like to point to these passages as proof of the rewriting of the Bible at later dates. From a liberal perspective, if the Bible records the name of a ruler before he was ever in power, it must have been added later. They would insist that some editor (or redactor) came along and added those details into the passages. Of course, this view undermines the authority of the Bible and can't be held in a consistent Christian's life.

There have also been many people in history who have claimed to be able to see the future. One of the most famous was Nostradamus. Nostradamus made many statements about the future, but they were quite cryptic and vague, written in four-line poetry. Many people claim that the prophecies have foretold events such as the rise of Hitler and the assassination of the Kennedy brothers, but the statements are typically interpreted after the events have already happened.

From an apologetics standpoint, we need to be careful not to think that the fulfilled biblical prophecies are a magic bullet that will bring everyone who hears them to faith in Christ. These truths can be used to confirm the supernatural nature of the Bible, but only God can open the eyes of those who are blind to His truth. We have the privilege of proclaiming the truth of God's Word (Romans 10) and watching as He uses that truth to draw people to Himself. You can boldly proclaim the truth of God's Word, including the clear future-telling that pointed to the coming of the Messiah who would save His people from their sin. Just as we can trust and confirm the accounts of Josiah and Cyrus, we know that Jesus has truly come to bring us new life.

For more information on this topic, see the Online Resource Page.

 **Studying God's Word**

How much does God know?

Take notes as you study the following passages.

1 Kings 13:1–7

2 Kings 23:15–20

 God vs. Nostradamus

Nostradamus was a sixteenth-century French astrologer who made predictions about the future. Use the information below to compare the predictions of Nostradamus to the predictions offered in the Bible.

Nostradamus Quatrain 10-72

> In the year 1999, in the seventh month,
> from the sky will come the great King of Terror,
> bringing back to life the great King of the Mongols.
> Before and after, Mars to reign by good fortune.

1. What event is this prophecy referring to?

2. Who are each of the people mentioned in the prophecy?

3. When will this prophecy be fulfilled?

4. After hearing the explanation of the prophecy, how does this compare to the prophecy of Josiah from 1 Kings 13?

Take notes as you study the following passages.

Isaiah 44:28–45:7

Ezra 1:1–4

 ## God's Word in the Real World

1. Does the fulfillment of the prophecies prove that the Bible is true?

2. In what way does this study encourage you?

3. If someone were to claim that the Bible only made specific predictions because later editors went back and filled in those details, how would you respond?

4. If someone were to claim that the Bible and the predictions made in it were no different than those of people like Nostradamus, how would you respond?

5. If you show someone the clear prophecy and its fulfillment, should you expect him to acknowledge God and his need for His salvation?

6. Do you trust these passages as prophesying the future?

Prayer Requests

7

God Answers Prayer

Key Passages

- Isaiah 36:13–22, 37:21–38; 2 Chronicles 32:9

What You Will Learn

- How Hezekiah depended on God.

- How God protected Jerusalem.

Lesson Overview

The southern kingdom of Judah was threatened by the mighty Assyrian empire. Trusting in the one true God for protection, good King Hezekiah went right to the Lord in prayer. God answered Hezekiah's prayer in an amazing way!

Memory Verse

Isaiah 53:6

All we like sheep have gone astray; we have turned, everyone, to his own way; and the Lord has laid on Him the iniquity of us all.

📖 Prepare to Learn

SCRIPTURAL BACKGROUND

As we begin this lesson, we are stepping back in time to the point where the kingdom was divided, but the focus is shifting to the Southern Kingdom. The first part of this quarter focused on how the Northern tribes turned from God and faced His judgment after He sent many prophets to warn them. Ultimately, the Assyrians conquered them and carried them off to foreign lands. As we talked about in Lesson 1, most of the kings of Judah led the people into idolatry, but a few sought to restore true worship of God.

One of these good kings was Hezekiah. Hezekiah was the thirteenth king in Judah and took the throne after his extremely wicked father, Ahaz. Ahaz had continued to worship false gods, even offering his children as sacrifices (2 Kings 16:1–4). He also looked to the king of Assyria for protection from the kings of Syria and Israel, offering him treasures from the house of God, rather than looking to God for deliverance (2 Kings 16:5–9). Hezekiah was nothing like his father—he "held fast to the Lord" and fought against the idolatry that plagued Judah (2 Kings 18:1–7). In fact, that passage tells us that "He trusted in the Lord God of Israel, so that after him was none like him among all the kings of Judah, nor who were before him."

Here is where we meet the prophet Isaiah for the first time. Most people would recognize Isaiah as an Old Testament prophet, but few know a lot about his ministry. Isaiah ministered for over 50 years in Judah over the span of four kings (Isaiah 1:1). He was a contemporary of Hosea and Micah and penned some of the most lamentable judgments against Judah, as well as descriptions of the glories of redemption through the coming Messiah. One of Isaiah's roles during this period of history was to deliver a message of assurance to Hezekiah.

As Hezekiah began his reign in the Southern Kingdom in 726 BC, the Northern Kingdom of Israel was about to fall to the captivity of the Assyrians under Tiglath Pileser III (the king Hezekiah's father Ahaz had made an alliance with) and Shalmaneser V. Next, Sennacherib took power in Assyria and began to expand his kingdom into Judah where Hezekiah had been reigning for 14 years (Isaiah 36:1). After taking several cities, Sennacherib sent to Jerusalem a delegation of officials, the Rabshakeh, along with a large portion of his army. The delegates delivered a message of boasting from their king to Hezekiah: Whether you seek help from Egypt or God, I will conquer you and your God cannot protect you (Isaiah 36).

When the message was delivered to Hezekiah, he was distraught and sent a message to Isaiah, calling for prayer for deliverance from God (Isaiah 37:1–4). When the messengers delivered the threat to Isaiah, God gave them a message to deliver to Hezekiah—don't fear Sennacherib; he will die in his own land (37:5–7). The Assyrian delegation returned to Jerusalem with another threat from Sennacherib and a boast against God (37:8–13). True to his character, Hezekiah cried out to God in a prayer that demonstrated his full reliance upon God, recognizing His sovereignty and mercy, and seeking God's glory in the matter. Hezekiah knew that God could prevail and that He would be glorified as all the kingdoms of the earth would hear how He had delivered Jerusalem (37:14–20).

God is merciful and gracious. In response to Hezekiah's humble request, God spoke a message of comfort and security through Isaiah. God would deliver Jerusalem from the Assyrians and strike down Sennacherib (Isaiah 37:21–35). God was about to display His sovereignty over the nations in a most dramatic way!

As Sennacherib's great army, which numbered more than 185,000, camped near Jerusalem, there was surely fear and rumors flashing throughout the city. In 2 Chronicles 32:1–23, we learn that Hezekiah also worked to prepare a defense of the city, but he was not trusting in the might of the men of the city for deliverance, but called the people to trust in "the Lord our God, to help us and to fight our battles." As God had promised, the Assyrian army did not even raise a shield or shoot an arrow at Jerusalem.

During the night, the Angel of the Lord moved through the camp of the Assyrians. As the camp awoke, they found quite a frightful scene—185,000 corpses lying in their midst! Imagine the fear and chaos that must have surged through the camp as those who were spared realized what had happened (Isaiah 37:36). Understanding his defeat, Sennacherib returned to Nineveh with his tail between his legs. Just as Isaiah had revealed, Sennacherib's sons killed him as he was worshipping before his god, Nisroch (37:37–38). This was just another display of the absolute power of the one true God over the demons behind the false gods worshipped by the heathen nations.

In this account, we see the greatness of God displayed in His control over the affairs of man and His kindness to answer the prayers of those who trust in Him and seek His glory. Hezekiah is surely an example we can look to, but God is the hero of the story. We can look to Hezekiah as an example of submitting to God in humility, not trusting in our own human strength, and seeking to bring God glory in all things. It is God who is the reason Hezekiah could do all of these things. God's glorious character is clearly on display in this account.

HISTORICAL/APOLOGETICS BACKGROUND

As you think about the structure of the Old Testament, it might be a little confusing. The account we are looking at in this lesson is actually referenced in at least three different places: Isaiah 36–37; 2 Kings 18–19; 2 Chronicles 32:1–23. In each we get a slightly different perspective, but all align and demonstrate the same truths about God's character. The political intrigue surrounding the transitions of the kings during this period is the stuff of an epic miniseries. Ahaz had been in league with kings of Assyria, Tiglath Pileser III and Shalmaneser V, and the son of the Assyrian king was now coming against the son of Ahaz. At the same time, Assyria was assaulting the Northern Kingdom while they were seeking help from other nations rather than God.

Hezekiah was the king reigning in the Southern Kingdom when the kings his father had cooperated with were sacking Samaria. Then, Shalmaneser's son Sennacherib moved on to wipe out Babylon and Egypt. So major portions of North Africa, Asia, and the Middle East were controlled by the Assyrian Empire. It was then that Sennacherib made his fatal mistake—he boasted against the Lord. God had ordained Sennacherib's reign and dominance of the people he and his fathers had conquered (Isaiah 9:11, 10:12–16, 37:26–27; Proverbs 21:1), but his pride brought judgment from God.

When you factor in the 30 other nations that were involved in these conflicts at this time and all of their leaders, you only begin to scratch the surface of the amazing tapestry of God's sovereignty in the affairs of the nations of the world over millennia. To even think of God as understanding and coordinating all of these events should drive us to our knees in praise of our awesome God. We can look to the words of God recorded in Isaiah 40 to get a sense of His awesome character and power:

> Behold, the nations are as a
> drop in a bucket,
> And are counted as the small
> dust on the scales;
> Look, He lifts up the isles as
> a very little thing.
> And Lebanon is not sufficient to burn,
> Nor its beasts sufficient for a
> burnt offering.
> All nations before Him are
> as nothing,
> And they are counted by
> Him less than nothing and
> worthless.
> To whom then will you
> liken God?
> Or what likeness will you
> compare to Him? (Isaiah
> 40:15–18)

 # Studying God's Word

What does prayer demonstrate?

Take notes as you study the following passage.
Isaiah 36:13–22

 # In God We Trust

The account of Hezekiah is recorded in three places in Scripture. Isaiah 36–37 is almost identical to 2 Kings 18–19 while 2 Chronicles 32 gives us some extra information. Use the following passages to answer the question about Hezekiah's dependence on God.

Read 2 Chronicles 32:1–8.

1. From this passage, describe how Hezekiah showed his dependence on God.

Read 2 Kings 19:1–20.

2. From this passage, describe how Hezekiah showed his dependence on God.

Take notes as you study the following passage.

Isaiah 37:21–38

2 Chronicles 32:9

 God's Word in the Real World

1. What does a sincere prayer to God, like Hezekiah's, demonstrate about a person?

2. What paradox do we find in praying to a God who is sovereign?

3. What is the connection between understanding God's character and offering prayers to Him?

4. Should we always expect a dramatic answer to prayer, as we saw with Hezekiah?

5. What passages of Scripture give you specific guidance about how to pray?

Prayer Requests

8

The Coming Ruler

Key Passages

- Micah 5:1–9, 7:18–20; 1 Peter 2:20–25

What You Will Learn

- How the prophecy in Micah connects to the person of Jesus.

- How God deals with our sins.

Lesson Overview

God had always planned that He would send a Savior to redeem fallen man. This plan is seen throughout the Old Testament and included Jesus Christ, the Son of God, to be born a man, live, die, and rise again so that all who would believe would be saved.

Memory Verse

Isaiah 53:6

All we like sheep have gone astray; we have turned, everyone, to his own way; and the Lord has laid on Him the iniquity of us all.

 **Prepare to Learn**

SCRIPTURAL BACKGROUND

The gospel—the good news of the redemption of sinners through the promised Messiah—is woven like a scarlet thread throughout the Bible, like an arrow pointing to something wonderful that would surely come to fulfillment. As we look at the prophet Micah, we will see that he was one of the prophets of God who had the privilege of announcing the coming Messiah.

Micah was a contemporary of Isaiah, ministering to both Israel to the north and Judah to the south. He preached in the days of Jotham, Ahaz, and Hezekiah, kings of Judah. His message concerned what he saw regarding Samaria and Jerusalem (Micah 1:1). He prophesied from around 760 to 710 BC. His proclamations and warnings were being sounded as Samaria fell to the Assyrians to the north in 721 BC.

Although Micah pronounced judgment on the people for their mistreatment of the poor (Micah 2:2), for false teachers (Micah 2:6), and for idolatry, he also spoke with hope of a light that would shine brightly into the future—a time when people would walk in the name of the Lord God forever and ever (Micah 4:5). His message of the future included revelations of the Messiah, the Savior—who He was and how He would be identified.

Let's look specifically at Micah 5:2. We see four characteristics here regarding the coming Messiah. First, the Messiah would be born in Bethlehem. Second, the Messiah would come from the tribe of Judah. Third, the Messiah would be eternal. And fourth, in Micah 5:4, the Messiah would act as a shepherd who would feed His flock. These prophecies were all fulfilled, and God confirmed the fulfillment of them in other parts of Scripture.

The first part of the prophecy, that the Messiah would be born in Bethlehem, is confirmed in several places in the New Testament writings. We read that Joseph went up from Nazareth with Mary, his betrothed wife who was with child, to the city of David, which is called Bethlehem (Luke 2:4–5). Luke also recorded that the angels brought good tidings to the shepherds that a Savior was born in the city of David—Bethlehem (Luke 2:10–12). So 700 years after Micah foretold the Messiah's birthplace, the Savior was born in Bethlehem.

The second thing Micah told about the Messiah (Micah 5:2) was that He would be from the tribe of Judah. We'll go back in the Old Testament to see one confirmation of this prophecy. When Jacob blessed his sons and grandsons, the connection between this coming Ruler and the tribe of

Judah was made. Jacob spoke of the scepter—a sign of kingship—not departing from Judah until Shiloh comes, the Ruler who will bring peace (Genesis 49:8–10). The author of Hebrews declared that the Lord arose from Judah (Hebrews 7:14). Looking forward to the book of Revelation, we read that Jesus the Messiah is referred to as the Lion of the tribe of Judah, the Root of David (Revelation 5:5). And finally, both genealogies of Christ show that He was from the tribe of Judah (Matthew 1:1–17; Luke 3:23–38).

The third characteristic described by Micah is the Messiah's eternality—His "goings forth are from old, from everlasting." Micah, by the inspiration of the Holy Spirit, revealed that the Messiah was and is eternal. This is surely a difficult concept to grasp. Jesus, as part of the Trinity, did not begin to exist when He was conceived by the Holy Spirit. He existed in triune communion with the Father and the Spirit before the universe was created—before there was time. The Apostle John opens his Gospel with confirmation of this truth about the Messiah. "In the beginning was the Word, and the Word was with God, and the Word was God. He was in the beginning with God" (John 1:1–2). Micah understood that the Messiah would be from everlasting to everlasting.

Fourthly, Micah described the Messiah as a shepherd who would "stand and feed His flock in the strength of the Lord" (Micah 5:4). The shepherd imagery of God and Jesus is found throughout Scripture (Psalm 23). And Jesus even referred to Himself as the "good shepherd" who gave His life for His sheep (John 10:11).

All of these characteristics of Jesus the Messiah are wonderful, and the Bible's confirmation of them gives us the assurance that Jesus Christ is the one prophesied by Micah.

One final truth from Micah about the Messiah is truly remarkable and very personal. Micah proclaimed that God would pardon iniquity and pass over the transgressions of His children. He would not retain His anger forever. He delights in mercy. God would have compassion on His children and cast all their sins into the depths of the sea (Micah 7:18–20). How would this be accomplished? Only through the finished work of Jesus Christ on the Cross. Peter described this in the New Testament when he said that Christ "bore our sins in His own body on the tree, that we, having died to sins, might live for righteousness" (1 Peter 2:24).

While Micah was looking forward to this Messiah and prophesying of Him by the power of God, we are able to look back and observe His finished work on the Cross—salvation and forgiveness for all who will repent, turn from their sins, and trust in this precious Messiah, Savior, Jesus Christ.

HISTORICAL/APOLOGETICS BACKGROUND

As we consider the role of the prophet, we often come across the word "predict." What comes to mind when you hear that someone made a prediction? Maybe you have made a prediction about who would win a contest or about when it would rain. What was that prediction based on? Would it be accurate to say that Micah made a prediction about the birthplace of Christ?

If we look up the word *predict* in Webster's Dictionary we find: "to declare or indicate in advance; *especially*: foretell on the basis of observation, experience, or scientific reason." The root of the word simply means "say before," but the common usage today would align itself more with foretelling based on an observation or experience, like forecasting the weather.

While Micah's statement about the birthplace of Christ was a prediction in the first sense of the definition above (declaring in advance), it cannot be explained by the second definition ("foretell on the basis of observation,

experience, or scientific reason"). This is because Micah was not analyzing patterns or basing his prophecy on his personal experiences and knowledge of the Messiah. He wasn't thinking that Jesus would *probably* be born in Bethlehem in Judah. No. It was the omniscient God who cannot lie who told Micah what was going to happen. Micah was merely passing the true Word of God along. The fulfillment of what Micah said was sure, not just probable. This was not a message from a weatherman, but from the God who controls the weather. And this surety is true of ALL the prophecies we find in Scripture.

Be aware that many modern Bible translations use a form of the word *predict* when talking about the sure proclamations of God. While this is not technically wrong according to the definition above, the wording can be misleading to many hearers if it is not carefully defined and explained as a sure foretelling of God's Word and His plan.

For more information on this topic, see the Online Resource Page.

Studying God's Word

Did Micah predict the birthplace of the Messiah?

Take notes as you study the following passage.

Micah 5:1–9

Micah's Prophecies

The prophet Micah offered hope to the Jewish people amidst his proclamation of judgment. These statements were made 700 years before the one he prophesied of was to come.

Use the following verses to connect the prophecies to their fulfillment in Jesus. Read each verse, identify which part of the prophecy it fulfills, then write the reference under the correct heading. Write a short description of how it is fulfilled. Be sure to read each verse in context. If you can, identify other passages that would confirm the fulfillment of the prophecies.

Genesis 49:10; John 10:11; John 1:1–2; Luke 2:10–12; Revelation 5:5

1. Out of Bethlehem shall come the one to be Ruler in Israel.

2. The Ruler will be from Judah, bringing peace to Israel.

3. The Ruler's nature is from everlasting (eternal).

4. The Ruler will feed His flock.

Take notes as you study the following passages.
Micah 7:18–20

1 Peter 2:20–25

 ## God's Word in the Real World

1. What was most helpful to you in our study today?

2. Have you been guilty of thinking about the Old Testament prophecies in the same way you think about predictions about the weather or who will win the Super Bowl? How has your thinking changed?

3. As you think about the idea of the scarlet thread of events pointing forward to Christ, how are you encouraged?

4. How could you use the ideas from this lesson to share the gospel with someone who is not trusting in Christ?

5. How could you use the ideas from this lesson to encourage another believer?

Prayer Requests

9

Messianic Prophecies

Key Passages

- Isaiah 7:10–17, 52:13–53:12; Matthew 1:18–25; 1 Peter 2:21–25

What You Will Learn

- The length of time between Isaiah's prophecies and Christ's life.

- Two prophecies specifically fulfilled by Jesus.

Lesson Overview

Isaiah foretold details of the Messiah's birth and death that only God could have revealed to His prophet. Their fulfillment, about 700 years later, reminds us that God's plan to send a Redeemer was in place before the beginning of time.

Memory Verse

Isaiah 53:6

All we like sheep have gone astray; we have turned, everyone, to his own way; and the Lord has laid on Him the iniquity of us all.

Prepare to Learn

SCRIPTURAL BACKGROUND

Have you ever tried to predict the future? How did that turn out for you? Sometimes, our guesses about what will happen in the future are based on sound reasoning and information, but even then, our predictions are not guaranteed to actually come to pass.

But this is not the case for our Creator—He knows all things past, present, and future. He alone is omniscient. God used prophets to speak for Him. And when He did, those things occurred. A true prophet was identified by the accuracy of his prophecy. If what he proclaimed did not come to pass, he was considered a false prophet (Deuteronomy 18:17–22).

Today, we'll see how God used His faithful prophet Isaiah. Isaiah spoke the words of God boldly and truthfully. Like the prophet Micah, Isaiah spoke about the coming Messiah in specific detail—700 years before He was born. We'll explore two of Isaiah's messianic prophecies, foretelling Christ's virgin birth and His death for our sin upon the Cross.

Isaiah 7:14 speaks of a virgin conceiving and bearing a Son whose name would be Immanuel. We later see a clear connection between Isaiah's words and the angel's message to Joseph in Matthew 1:20–25, where Isaiah's prophecy is repeated and

the name of Immanuel is translated as "God with us." The virgin, Mary, would bring forth a Son by the power of the Holy Spirit. Jesus would be fully God and fully man (John 1:14). The prophecy of Isaiah 7:14, proclaimed almost 700 years before Jesus was born, was fulfilled and recorded in the New Testament.

The second prophecy from Isaiah that pointed forward to the Messiah came much later in his ministry. In Isaiah 52:13–53:12, Isaiah spoke of the suffering Servant who would be beaten, despised, mocked, and rejected. This Man would be wounded for our transgressions and bruised for our iniquities. He would become the offering for sin and die in the place of sinners.

Only the hardhearted can read this passage and not recognize the suffering and death of Jesus during the final days of His life on earth. In fact, anecdotes tell of Christians asking Jews to listen to this passage and to identify who is being described. As they acknowledge it describes Jesus's death, they are then shocked to learn that these words were spoken by the Jewish prophet Isaiah in the Old Testament—700 years before Jesus's birth.

For Christians, these words from Isaiah should shock us as well, but in a different way. We should be shocked to realize how much Jesus had to suffer for our sins. Go back and read Isaiah 52:13–53:12 again. Think about your role in why Jesus was tortured and crucified. Remember that the Father had to crush His Son so that you would not face His wrath in hell. As you were a sheep wandering after your own desires, Jesus was led as a lamb to be slaughtered on your behalf. Now take a moment to read 1 Peter 2:21–25 and notice the language that Peter is borrowing from Isaiah.

Isaiah's Prophecy	Connections in 1 Peter 2
53:5—He was wounded for our transgressions	2:21—Christ suffered for believers
53:9—He did no violence, nor was any deceit in His mouth	2:22—Christ committed no sin or deceit
53:7—He opened not His mouth	2:23—Christ did not return the reviling He received
53:4–5—He bore our grief and was wounded for our transgressions	2:24—Christ bore our sins on the Cross that we might be healed
53:6—We all like sheep have gone astray	2:25—We have all gone our own way, like sheep

Jesus has fulfilled the messianic prophecies delivered by Isaiah. What an amazing Savior we serve! He alone is worthy of our worship and praise. He is the only one who can save us from our sin.

HISTORICAL/APOLOGETICS BACKGROUND

Isaiah was a prophet during the reigns of Uzziah, Jotham, Ahaz, and Hezekiah in the Southern Kingdom of Judah. His ministry lasted from about 760 to 700 BC and was primarily focused on Judah. His prophecies not only included calls to repentance from sin but also presented the hope of a future deliverer—the Savior and Messiah who would one day come.

We've said that Isaiah's prophecy of the virgin birth was 700 years before Jesus's birth. We know this timeframe to be true because the Bible says Isaiah spoke his words to King Ahaz (7:1, 7:3, 7:10), who ruled in Judah from 742–726 BC. Isaiah's ministry continued into the reign of King Hezekiah who ruled from 726–698 BC. We read in Lesson 7 that Judah was attacked by the Assyrians in 712 BC during the fourteenth year of Hezekiah's reign (Isaiah 36:1). The prophecies of Isaiah recorded in chapter 39 and following were delivered after Samaria fell to the Assyrians and when the Babylonian empire was on the rise. The prophecies from this later section of the book of Isaiah were most likely delivered around the same time since there are no clear time markers in the text. This places Isaiah's description of the Messiah's suffering and death more than 700 years before it happened.

One of the most powerful confirmations of the truthfulness of Scripture comes in the fulfillment of specific prophecies made well in advance of the actual events. The foreshadowing of Jesus's death in Isaiah 53 was a demonstration of God's sovereignty and omniscience as we recognize the precise fulfillment in the crucifixion recorded in the New Testament. God is the only one who knows the future with absolute certainty.

Although we can make plans, we can't know what will happen tomorrow. In fact, to presume to know our future is to set ourselves in a place that only God should sit (James 4:13–16). God alone is omniscient. He alone knows the future. And He alone directs our steps (Proverbs 16:9). His counsel will stand in spite of the plans we make (Proverbs 19:21). Confidence in His sovereignty and His omniscience will lead to confidence in His Word. That confidence can lead us to humbly submit to His Word and the truths it reveals—leading to an assurance of eternal life through the Lord Jesus Christ.

For more information on this topic, see the Online Resource Page.

 Studying God's Word

Why is the name Immanuel important?

Take notes as you study the following passages.

Isaiah 7:10–17

Matthew 1:18–25

The Old Testament Cross

Both Micah and Isaiah were prophets who foretold the events of the coming of the Messiah—covering His birth, death, and beyond. Even though the use of crucifixion was not known until much later than the time when Isaiah wrote, it is clearly in view in Isaiah 52–53.

Read Isaiah 52:13–53:12 carefully and thoughtfully. In the sections below, write a summary of what the passage teaches about the person and work of Jesus, especially on the Cross.

1. How is the Messiah's appearance described?

2. How did people treat Him?

3. What responses did He make?

4. How did He die?

5. How was God the Father involved?

6. How is sin discussed in this passage?

7. What language is used to describe the atonement for sin?

8. How do you know that Jesus has borne your sins on the Cross?

Take notes as you study the following passage.

1 Peter 2:21–25

_____

_____

_____

_____

God's Word in the Real World

1. How does God's omniscience help us understand the topic we have been discussing today?

2. Do the fulfilled prophecies in Isaiah prove that the Bible is true?

3. Isaiah 52–53 is written in both future and past tense language when it describes Jesus (compare 53:3 contains "is" and "was"). Why could Isaiah speak in this way in this section of Scripture?

4. What have you learned or been reminded of in today's lesson that helps you to trust God more?

5. How can you see yourself using this information in evangelistic ways?

Prayer Requests

10
God Warns Judah

Key Passages

- Jeremiah 2:4–8, 3:6–10, 4:1–2, 4:5–12, 5:18–19

What You Will Learn

- Why God was angry with Judah.

- How God judged Judah.

Lesson Overview

God was angry with Judah because of their many years of idolatry. Just like Israel, He would judge them by sending a nation from the north to capture them and destroy their land.

Memory Verse

Isaiah 53:6

All we like sheep have gone astray; we have turned, everyone, to his own way; and the Lord has laid on Him the iniquity of us all.

Prepare to Learn

SCRIPTURAL BACKGROUND

Jeremiah is often referred to as the "weeping prophet" because of the nature of his ministry, and the label fits. Jeremiah primarily prophesied in the Southern Kingdom of Judah during the final decades of that kingdom. The 10 tribes of the Northern Kingdom had been carried away, and the region was repopulated with Gentiles who intermarried with the Jews left behind. In the South, there was a series of good and bad kings.

Jeremiah was one of the prophets God sent to warn Judah, and his messages began during the reign of Josiah (Jeremiah 1:2, 3:6). Josiah was the sixteenth king of Judah and was one of the best kings. He was working to rid Judah of idol worship, turning them back to worshipping the one true God (2 Kings 22–23). Jeremiah was not the first prophet to be sent to Judah; Micah, Isaiah, Joel, Obadiah, and others preceded him, and he was a contemporary of Daniel, Ezekiel, Habakkuk, and Zephaniah. God sent warnings to Judah through all of these men. Judah had periods of restoration, like the period when Isaiah was prophesying under King Hezekiah, but they were constantly backsliding just as Israel had done (Jeremiah 3:6–10). Jeremiah gave the final warnings of the coming destruction to Judah. He called for repentance and for the people to turn back to God. Because of their unfaithfulness to God, Judah was described as an adulterous wife, just like her sister Israel.

For their adulterous idolatry, God pronounced through Jeremiah that a lion from the north would come and lay siege to their city (Jeremiah 4:5–8). Judah was to be wiped out for their continual wickedness, despite the short periods of correct worship (2 Kings 23:26). Jeremiah foretold the coming destruction of Judah and Jerusalem at the hands of the Babylonians. This destruction would come in three phases. We'll get to that in the next lesson.

Because he was constantly and harshly warning the kings of coming judgment and calling them to repentance, Jeremiah was persecuted. During his ministry, Jeremiah faced death threats (Jeremiah 11:18–23, 26:8), was beaten and placed in stocks (20:2), had his writings burned (36:23–26), was thrown into a miry dungeon (38:6), was carried away captive in chains (40:1), and faced many other trials.

Frankly, it is all a little depressing. But the judgment he was proclaiming was deserved as Judah had persisted in following after false gods rather than the God who had delivered them from Egypt and established them in the Promised Land. God judged the people of Judah, and He warned them that because they had forsaken Him and served foreign gods, they would be taken hostage and serve foreigners in another land (Jeremiah 5:19). As bleak as that future appeared, God also gave the people the message that they would not be completely wiped out, but a remnant would turn back to God and cry for relief (Jeremiah 5:18). God made it clear that the captivity described in Jeremiah chapter 5 would only last 70 years (Jeremiah 25:12).

In spite of all the warnings and proclamations of coming disaster, there was also a foreshadowing of eternal hope. Jeremiah spoke of the days when the Lord would raise to David a Branch of righteousness—a King who would reign and prosper. He would be called "THE LORD OUR RIGHTEOUSNESS" (Jeremiah 23:5–6). This was a foreshadowing of the coming Messiah.

We can live in this same hope as we face periods of conflict or brokenness in our lives, families, country, and world. Like Judah in Jeremiah's time, we live in a world cursed because of our sin, our idolatry, our unrepentant hearts. The hope Jeremiah spoke of is the same for us. Jesus Christ will come to restore all things one day. He will restore this broken creation. Jesus Christ offers a plan of redemption for sinners through His life, death, and Resurrection that can assure those who repent and believe a place with Him in eternity. This is our blessed Redeemer. This is our blessed hope.

HISTORICAL/APOLOGETICS BACKGROUND

As we look at the opening passage of Jeremiah, we have a clear timeframe for the ministry of Jeremiah. He was a young man when God first called him to be a prophet to the nations (Jeremiah 1:1–8), probably in his twenties, and possibly as old as 90 when he died. He began prophesying in 630 BC, the thirteenth year of the reign of Josiah (Jeremiah 25:3), and the closing passages recount the release of Jehoiachin in 562 BC—indicating a span of 68 years of ministry. Unlike most of the prophets, Jeremiah was alive to actually see his prophecies of Jerusalem's destruction come to fulfillment, living through those horrid days when kings were captured and the city and Temple were burned and leveled. We will see as we continue our lessons that Jeremiah's role to Judah was not finished. His influence would continue into the 70 years of captivity that he had prophesied.

We have looked at some very specific prophecies from both Isaiah (last week) and Jeremiah. The statements they made were proclaiming in very particular detail what would happen in the future. Many people doubt that these statements are actually prophecies of the future. Rather, they say that an editor added those things back into the text after they had already happened. They doubt that the prophets really received messages from God and recorded what He told them. They doubt the absolute truthfulness and authority of the Bible.

As you face skeptics who want to attack the authority and authenticity of God's Word—whether inside or outside the church—remember, the Word of God speaks for itself. Show your friends where God's Word speaks specifically about the topic you are discussing. This way, those you are talking with will be forced to combat the words you show them in the Bible. Most skeptics are quick to deny man's opinions but will find it more difficult to deny the Bible and the very words it contains.

We can cling to the truth proclaimed in Scripture. There we find the knowledge of who God is, what He has done for us in Christ, and how He works in us through the Holy Spirit. As we study God's Word, we trust that the God of the universe is speaking and that we have the privilege of receiving His words. We must heed the warnings, obey the commands, and trust in the promises, knowing that we are submitting to the Creator of the universe who has graciously saved us from our sinful selves and adopted us into His family.

For more information on this topic, see the Online Resource Page.

 Studying God's Word

Where do idols come from?

Take notes as you study the following passages.

Jeremiah 2:4–8, 3:6–10, 4:1–2

 Idols of the Heart

Answer the following questions about the passage below. Remember that repeated words and phrases can help to identify key ideas in any biblical passage.

Read Ezekiel 14:1–7.

1. Identify three key ideas about idols from the passage.

   a.

   b.

   c.

Read James 1:13–15.

2. Do you recognize any of your key ideas in this passage even though the word "idol" is not used? Explain the connection.

Take notes as you study the following passages.

Jeremiah 4:5–12, 5:18–19

_____

_____

 God's Word in the Real World

1. God called the people of Judah to repent of their idolatry. What would that repentance have looked like?

2. We learned today that idols are actually manifestations of desires that we have in our own hearts. Can any of you put your finger on idols in your own heart that have led you into sin?

3. In Psalm 139, David praises God for His goodness and closes with a request for God to help him understand his heart, exposing any anxiety or wickedness (Psalm 139:23–24). How could this be used as a prayer to help you identify any idols you have set up in your heart?

4. How does today's lesson point you toward the need for a Savior to free you from sin?

 Prayer Requests

_____

_____

11
God Judges Judah

Key Passages

- 2 Chronicles 36:1–21; Jeremiah 5:18–19

What You Will Learn

- How the Babylonians treated the Israelites.

- How God judged Judah's sin.

Lesson Overview

For hundreds of years God warned Judah and called them to repent through His prophets. They didn't turn from evil, so God used Babylon to destroy Judah. They killed most of the people, destroyed the Temple of God, and took survivors to Babylon as slaves.

Memory Verse

Isaiah 53:6

All we like sheep have gone astray; we have turned, everyone, to his own way; and the Lord has laid on Him the iniquity of us all.

📖 Prepare to Learn

SCRIPTURAL BACKGROUND

God hates sin. We can have no doubt about that after looking at the calls of the prophets for Israel and Judah to repent. As we walk through biblical history, we have already seen God's judgment on Israel—they were wiped out by the Assyrians back in 721 BC. Now we look to the fall of Judah, beginning in 607 BC. Jeremiah was one of the last prophets to call Judah to repent, but they continued to rebel against God—and now it was their turn to face judgment. The fall of Judah and Jerusalem to the south was very similar to the fall of Israel and Samaria to the north. Despite numerous warnings from prophets over many centuries, the kings and people continually sought to worship false gods (with a few exceptions). Through the prophecies of Isaiah and Jeremiah, God had finally fixed a day of judgment for Judah. The lion from the north (Jeremiah 4:5–8), Babylon, was about to attack and carry away the rest of the Jewish nation.

Just as God used Assyria to deliver judgment to His people in Israel about 125 years earlier, He was about to send Babylon to deliver judgment to Judah. Babylon's king at this time was Nebuchadnezzar. This wicked king was the one God chose to bring His judgment to Judah.

Nebuchadnezzar was the son of the previous Babylonian king, Nabopolassar. God used King Nabopolassar to destroy and conquer the Assyrians in 626 BC. This was after the Assyrians had destroyed the Northern nation of Israel. God would now use Babylon again—this time to bring judgment on Judah.

Historically, one strategy for gaining complete power over an enemy was to remove most of the conquered nation to other lands. If you remember from the lesson on the fall of Israel, this was what the Assyrians did to the Jews in the Northern nation of Israel. In our account today, we will see that the Babylonians were to do the same. In order to completely weaken the nation of Judah, they would move the people out and settle them in other nations.

The destruction of Judah by Babylon occurred over three phases. The city of Jerusalem and the Temple were not totally destroyed until the third phase.

During the first phase (607 BC), Nebuchadnezzar moved King Jehoiakim and many of the princes and nobles out of Judah as described in Daniel 1:1–4. His goal was to train them to be good Babylonians and to put them into service in his court. In the second phase (599 BC), Nebuchadnezzar took King Jehoiachin captive and moved the king and thousands of others to Babylon (Jeremiah 52:28; 2 Kings 24:10–16). These were devastating events for the people of Judah. But the worst was yet to come.

Now came phase three. Imagine yourself as one of the Jewish inhabitants of Jerusalem in 588 BC. Nebuchadnezzar had been harassing your nation for almost 20 years, and now his army was camped around the city again! Would you survive this time? Would you be taken away this time? Would you be separated from your family? Or worse yet, would you have to watch them die at the hands of the Babylonians? All of this and more did occur when Babylon finally came to put an end to Judah.

A clear picture of the devastation caused by this judgment is found in 2 Chronicles 36:15–21. Because the people had mocked God, His warnings, and His messengers, because they had despised His words and scoffed at His prophets, the wrath of the Lord came against them. The Babylonians, here called the Chaldeans, came into Jerusalem. They killed the young men and had no compassion on the men, women, aged, or weak. All the articles from the house of God were taken to Babylon. They burned the house of God, burned the palaces, destroyed all the precious possessions, and broke down the wall of Jerusalem. And those citizens of Jerusalem who were not killed during this rampage were moved far away to Babylon and became servants there.

But in spite of the devastation of Judah and Israel, all was not lost! God already had a plan to restore Jerusalem, to rebuild the Temple, and to continue the line of Abraham through King David and on to the coming Messiah.

HISTORICAL/APOLOGETICS BACKGROUND

As mentioned earlier, the history of the final fall of Judah and Jerusalem is a bit complex, coming in three phases over 19 years and involving four different kings of Judah. The first phase occurred after the good King Josiah (who was the sixteenth ruler in the Southern Kingdom) died. His son Jehoahaz ruled for only three months (2 Kings 23:30–32). Then, Pharaoh Necho from Egypt captured him and set another son of Josiah, Jehoiakim, over Judah, making him pay tribute to Egypt (2 Kings 23:33–35). As had been the pattern, these two sons of Josiah did what was evil in the sight of the Lord. Judah was beginning to crumble, and the first phase of her destruction was about to begin.

The Babylonian leader Nebuchadnezzar defeated the Egyptians and took control of all of Egypt's lands, including Judah (2 Kings 24:7). So, for the first three years of his reign, Jehoiakim was subject to Egypt, but for the last eight he was subject to Babylon (2 Kings 23:36–24:4). In 607 BC,

Nebuchadnezzar came to Babylon and defeated Jehoiakim, who had rebelled against him (2 Kings 24:1–2). The Babylonians carried away some of the articles of the Temple and many of the young nobles, including Daniel (Daniel 1:1–4). This began the 70 years of captivity that Jeremiah had prophesied (Jeremiah 25:11).

The second phase of the captivity happened about seven years later. Nebuchadnezzar had restored Jehoiakim to the throne in Jerusalem, but he later died and his body was thrown outside the gates of the city (Jeremiah 22:18–19). Jehoiakim's son Jehoiachin (also called Jeconiah or Coniah) reigned for three months after his father's death. In 599 BC, the Babylonians returned and carried away more than 3,000 Jews, including Jehoiachin, along with all of the articles of the Temple (2 Kings 24:10–16; Jeremiah 52:28). The brother of Jehoiakim, Zedekiah, was set up as the puppet king under the control of Nebuchadnezzar. His reign extended from 599 until 588.

588 BC marked the third phase of Judah's captivity. Nebuchadnezzar returned and utterly destroyed Jerusalem and the Temple and the people were either killed, taken away into captivity, or left to tend the land for the remainder of the 70 years (2 Kings 25:8–21; 2 Chronicles 36:15–21). It would be another 49 years before Cyrus would allow the captives to begin returning to rebuild Jerusalem. So the 70 years of captivity, which will be discussed in the next lesson, lasted from 607 BC with the first deportation by Nebuchadnezzar until 537 BC when Cyrus fulfilled the prophecies Jeremiah and Isaiah made hundreds of years prior. In an interesting parallel, the return to rebuild Jerusalem also happened in three phases . . . but we will have to save that for another lesson.

For more information on this topic, see the Online Resource Page.

 Three Steps to Destruction

In this activity you will be reading through 2 Kings 23:26–25:12 and looking at the sequence and timing of events around the fall of Judah and Jerusalem. For each of the kings below, record the details that you find in the text as indicated, noting their relationship to Josiah, length of reign, and the acts described.

Preliminary

King Josiah (died in 610 BC)

    Reign:

    Acts:

    Oppressor/Acts:

King Jehoahaz

    Reign:

    Acts:

    Oppressor/Acts:

Phase 1

King Jehoiakim

    Reign:

    Acts:

    Oppressor/Acts:

Phase 2

King Jehoiachin

    Reign:

    Acts:

    Oppressor/Acts:

Phase 3

King Zedekiah

    Reign:

    Acts:

    Oppressor/Acts:

Studying God's Word

Take notes as you study the following passages.

2 Chronicles 36:1–21

Jeremiah 5:18–19

God's Word in the Real World

1. What have you learned (or had confirmed) about Scripture as we studied this passage today?

2. If you find yourself thinking, "I can't believe the people of Judah saw what happened to Israel and didn't turn to God," what are you forgetting about mankind?

3. What do the actions of the Babylonians tell us about the nature of mankind?

4. What future events does our study today set up?

Prayer Requests

12
Seventy Years

Key Passages

- Jeremiah 25:1–14, 29:1–20; Daniel 1:1, 9:1–2

What You Will Learn

- The length of the captivity of Judah in Babylon.

- What prophecies Jeremiah made during the captivity

Lesson Overview

God finally judged Judah through King Nebuchadnezzar of Babylon. The survivors of the Babylonian attack were taken to Babylon to serve as slaves. However, God did not leave them without hope. God spoke through His prophet Jeremiah and revealed that the captivity would be 70 years and then their faithful God would return them home again.

Memory Verse

Isaiah 53:6

All we like sheep have gone astray; we have turned, everyone, to his own way; and the Lord has laid on Him the iniquity of us all.

Prepare to Learn

SCRIPTURAL BACKGROUND

For years Jeremiah had issued warnings to the people of Judah. The lion from the north (Jeremiah 4:5–8), Babylon, would come and wipe out the nation. Judah was warned to repent of their evil ways. Jeremiah implored them to give up their false gods, so that God's anger would not be provoked against them. Yet they did not listen to the Lord (Jeremiah 25:4–7). God's anger was finally unleashed against them through King Nebuchadnezzar and the Babylonians. The day of judgment had come for Judah. In fact, Nebuchadnezzar and the Babylonians destroyed Jerusalem, burning the city and the Temple to the ground as well as destroying the city wall and killing many of the inhabitants (2 Kings 25:8–10). During this destruction, Jeremiah continued to be a key figure in the Jewish community along with two other prophets of God, Daniel and Ezekiel.

Up to this point, Jeremiah had served many different roles as a prophet of God. He proclaimed judgments against the kings and people of Judah (Jeremiah 2–4). He called the people to repentance (Jeremiah 4:14–18). He promised that God would not completely destroy them and would one day restore His people (Jeremiah 5:18).

Today, we will see that God required even more of His prophet, Jeremiah. God gave him words to speak concerning future events and to bring specific commands to God's people (Jeremiah 29). Jeremiah brought these particular prophecies on behalf of God while the people were in captivity in Babylon.

The first prophecy concerning future events had to do with how long God's people would be captive to the Babylonians. We read about this in Jeremiah 25. Jeremiah gave this prophecy in "the fourth year of Jehoiakim" (Jeremiah 25:1)—before Babylon's initial invasion. Jeremiah recorded here for the first time that God would remove the voice of mirth and gladness from the people who would now serve the king of Babylon for 70 years (Jeremiah 25:10–11). Jeremiah also assured the people that when the 70 years of desolation were completed, Babylon would be judged for their iniquity (Jeremiah 25:12).

Once the captivity of Judah began, the people no doubt began to listen to and believe Jeremiah. The prophecies concerning their destruction by Babylon had occurred exactly as he had predicted, and the 70 years of captivity would surely follow. In fact, the prophet Daniel—himself a victim of the Babylonian deportation—confirmed his confidence in Jeremiah's 70-year prophecy as evidenced by his own writing (Daniel 9:1–2). Another confirmation to this important prophecy appears in 2 Chronicles 36. The Scriptures mention that those who escaped the sword and were carried away to Babylon were made servants of that kingdom. And while they were captive, the land they left—Judah—would lay desolate for 70 years (2 Chronicles 36:20–21).

So God used Jeremiah to speak of the future—that the Jewish people would be captive in Babylon for 70 years. But God was also to use Jeremiah to instruct His people even as they lived as servants in Babylon. In a letter to the priests, the prophets, and all the people carried away by King Nebuchadnezzar, Jeremiah reminded the people that it was the Lord who caused them to be carried away as captives (Jeremiah 29:4). Because they would be there so long, God commanded them to build houses, plant gardens, take wives, and start families so they would continue to increase in number (29:5–6). This would set the foundation for a return to Jerusalem at the end of the 70 years—a godly remnant who would repopulate Jerusalem and continue the line that would ultimately lead to the Messiah.

God continued speaking to them through Jeremiah as a faithful Father would. God reassured His children that, after the 70 years were completed, He would indeed cause them to return to the land He had led them away from. The Lord was looking forward to restoring the worship in Jerusalem and to renewing the people

in right worship (Jeremiah 29:10–14). The words of Jeremiah to the exiles were words of true hope, filled with the language of certainty—God would bring these things to pass.

God's commands had been given, and the people had hope. But Jeremiah again had to give warning to the people in exile—warning against false prophets in their midst who strove to deceive the people with lies. These prophets claimed their dreams were of the Lord and dared to speak in His name. The Lord warned the people that these false prophets had not come in His name (Jeremiah 29:8–9). The Lord advised that those prophets were not to be trusted or listened to. The false prophets would deal with the consequences—God's punishment and curse (Jeremiah 29:21–32).

And so the people waited in hope—true hope—given to them by a proven prophet of God, Jeremiah. They would be led by God back to Jerusalem after the appointed time. They knew that throughout the entire history of Israel, God had been directing their steps. From calling Moses to lead the people out of Egypt to the installing of the first king—from the constant rebellions to the capture of Israel by the Assyrians and the capture of Judah by the Babylonians—God had been in control. God was orchestrating their lives and future through His providential care and sovereign grace.

HISTORICAL/APOLOGETICS BACKGROUND

If you walk into your local neighborhood Christian bookstore, you will likely find plaques and trinkets inscribed with Scripture. Often, there will be a single verse or even part of a verse with a picture. But what about the context of the passage? If we only read a verse or part of a verse, we have no context. We must be very careful to not make claims about a passage of Scripture that the author never intended or that would not be faithful to the true meaning of God's Word.

One of the classic examples of taking a verse completely out of context is found in Jeremiah's letter to the exiles. If you just read Jeremiah 29:11, you might think this is a wonderful promise to claim. God seems to be telling you that He has a wonderful plan for your life—a life of peace with a hopeful future.

So how do we know to whom this verse applies? If we apply the hermeneutical skills we have been using to examine Scripture, all we need to do is ask a few questions. Who is writing this letter? Jeremiah. Who is he writing to? The captives in exile in Babylon. Who is the you in verse 11? It is the captives mentioned in verse 4. When will this peaceful prospering begin? Only after 70 years of captivity in Babylon.

So why doesn't anyone claim verse 10 as his life verse? What about verse 17? Could the Apostle Paul have said that Jeremiah 29:11 characterized his life? While all of God's Word is profitable for us (2 Timothy 3:16–17) and the things written in the Old Testament are for our instruction (Romans 15:4) not every verse applies directly to us today. We cannot simply insert our name into a verse wherever we want, nor can we deny a verse that clearly applies to us. We must look to rightly divide (accurately handle) God's Word and faithfully present what it says (2 Timothy 2:15).

Other clear passages in Scripture talk about God's plans for His children. Romans 8 clearly talks about God's care and love for each believer and gives a firm promise that He will work all things together for good and conform them to the image of Christ until the day of their glorification (Romans 8:28–30). We have confident hope in the promises of God because of His faithful character. We have salvation from our sins because of what Christ has done on our behalf. And we have power to live our lives, whether in peaceful or tumultuous circumstances, through the Holy Spirit.

For more information on this topic, see the Online Resource Page.

# Studying God's Word

Why is context so important?

Take notes as you study the following passages.
Jeremiah 25:1-14

Daniel 1:1

Daniel 9:1-2

Is Context King?

Walking into a local Christian bookstore, you are likely to find plaques and pictures with various verses inscribed on them. You might find the same visiting the website of a celebrity who is a Christian. However, these verses are often isolated from their context. The two verses below are popular in such instances. Your job is to examine the context of these verses and decide whether they are being used in a way that is faithful to God's intention for the passage.

Scenario 1

In a graduation speech at a Christian school, a young lady quotes Jeremiah 29:11. She tells her classmates that they can know God will prosper them because of this promise.

1. Who is the intended audience of this verse?

2. How was this message delivered?

3. Jeremiah 29:12 talks about a future time using "then" to point forward. When is this time?

4. Who is the "you" in verse 11 referring to? Is the "you" plural or singular?

5. Is the promise in verses 17–18 given to the same group?

6. Could this verse be applied to every Christian around the world at any time? (Consider Paul's life or believers in prison camps in North Korea.)

7. Did the young lady use this verse faithfully?

Scenario 2

A boxer enters the ring with Philippians 4:13 embroidered on his robe, believing that God will be on his side and strengthen him as he fights.

8. What is the "all" referring to in this verse?

9. What if the other guy came out with the same verse on his robe?

10. Is this promise intended for a boxing match?

11. Is this boxer faithfully and accurately handling God's Word?

Take notes as you study the following passages.

Jeremiah 29:1–20

 God's Word in the Real World

1. We have looked at many interconnected pieces of Scripture in this lesson and the last. How do these intricate connections in different books of the Bible and the people described in its pages give you assurance of the truthfulness of Scripture?

2. How can you use the faithfulness of God in fulfilling His promises, of judgment or restoration, as a source of hope?

3. After discussing the use of Jeremiah 29:11 and Philippians 4:13, how should you react when people use (or misuse) these verses, or others, in the future?

4. How does examining the Scripture in its historical context help you to understand God more fully and your place in the full scope of His redemptive history?

5. How can you use what we have learned today to offer encouragement to other believers or to share the gospel with someone?

Prayer Requests